ZACK MONTOYA

WAGON MOUND'S

PATRIARCH

BY

MANUEL B. ALCON

Order this book online at www.trafford.com
or email orders@trafford.com

Most Trafford titles are also available at major online book retailers.

Note for Librarians: A cataloguing record for this book is available from Library
and Archives Canada at www.collectionscanada.ca/amicus/index-e.html

Printed in Victoria, BC, Canada.

ISBN:978-1-4251-8905-1 (Soft)

*Our mission is to efficiently provide the world's finest, most comprehensive
book publishing service, enabling every author to experience success.
To find out how to publish your book, your way, and have it available
worldwide, visit us online at www.trafford.com*

Trafford rev. 9/28/2009

 www.trafford.com

North America & international
toll-free: 1 888 232 4444 (USA & Canada)
phone: 250 383 6864 ♦ fax: 812 355 4082

THIS BOOK IS DEDICATED TO ZACK'S CHILDREN AS WELL AS TO ALL HIS
FRIENDS AND HIS READERS.

PREFACE

I have known Zack for as long as I can remember. I have always admired him and have used him as my model in many respects. He and I have many things in common besides he is my favorite first cousin.

Some of the similarities are: Both of us have four children, three girls and one boy. Both boys went to college and are now Engineer technicians.

My youngest girl is a teacher as are Zack's three daughters.

We took the same course in history with the same professor at the same college. We have in common one set of grandparents. Both of us have many things in common. Both of us have done woodwork, automotive work, have been service station attendants and have taught school.

We have both taught history and social science although not in the same school. Both of us have been Principals as well as Superintendents of Independent School Districts.

Both have celebrated our 50th wedding anniversary although not on the same date or year. We have been close to each other and attended the same university where we got our B.A. and M.A. degrees.

Both served during World War II. He served in the U.S. Army and I served in the U.S. Navy.

Some of our differences are in our age, experiences, and characteristics. He is a strict disciplinarian with much patience and uses common sense as well as humor which I greatly admire and haven't been able to imitate him there.

I will add comments from many people that have worked, played and suffered with him. Frankly, I believe they can express themselves better than I can in that they have known him more intimately than I have. I have worked with him as his principal a short time before he retired and the people who vouched for him in the latter part of this book have done a better job of describing Zack. I agree with all the comments in the letters which his neighbors and friends have taken the time to write, recommending him for the NEA-NM Hall of Fame.

It is my wish that my readers will learn some history from the information given here. And like Zack says, "Laughter is one of the best medicines and it is free so enjoy life while you can"

He has countless humorous anecdotes and can make one laugh with his quick wit.

He is a devout Christian and lives his life accordingly, and as he would end his day's work with the wish of "God Bless us all always",.

THE LIFE STORY OF ZACK MONTOYA
WRITTEN BY M. B. ALCON

Zack was born on November 5, 1913 on a Wednesday to the union of Esequiel Montoya and Carlota Valdez Montoya. His grandparents on his father side were Francisco Montoya and Jesusita Apodaca Montoya. On his mother's side, his grandfather was Antonio Valdez and Clarita Stein Valdez.Claritas Parents came from Germany. Zack's father was raised at El Coyote, now called Rainsville. When they moved to Wagon Mound, his trade was meat cutter in a store. Zack was the second born in a family of ten. He was baptized Zacarias.

His family consisted of his father, mother and sisters and brothers. They are in the order of birth: Clara, Zack, Esequiel, Lydia, Sara, Edward, Helen, Antonio, Stellita, and Adolfo. Antonito and Stellita, both died when they were infants. Adolfo was born at the Paltinghe Ranch and was in the U.S. Army during the Second World War where he was mortally wounded by a Japanese sniper's bullet while he was on duty at Luzon, Philippine Islands.

Zack was born at Wagon Mound. Later, the family moved to a ranch on the road to Roy. The first school he attended was a rural school. The school was at Los Paises. He remembers his first teachers, Maria Tejada, Floripa Chavez and Facundo Fernandez. The teachers boarded with the neighbors. The teachers were teaching in English but they had to translate into Spanish so that the children would understand what was going on. At this time there were 64 school districts in Mora County. Each little school house had its own teacher. Some were two room schools. Most of the rural schools were a one room school.

This specific school was one of the one room schools. He was taught phonics and the school was bilingual. (English and Spanish) Lessons were in English and they learned to read English although most of the time, if not all the time, they didn't know what they were reading. They learned by memorizing words. At home and at the ranch only Spanish was spoken. Everyone spoke it in this, his world. His first teachers were his parents who taught him the virtues of life such as honesty, hard work, manners, and other virtues which were very reliable to all.

His parents planted beans, corn and other staples needed to survive. They had cows as well as other farm animals and with the products from these animals and the crops which they raised they were self sustained. For luxuries such as sugar, flour and coffee, as well as for clothing, they went to Wagon Mound, which was the closest town to their ranch. Wagon Mound at this time was a small village but it had stores, post office, a drug store, four bars, and other buildings which made life more comfortable.

Beans were the main crop and at harvest time the parents would take a trip to Wagon Mound to trade beans, wool and other things for those (necessities) they couldn't or didn't produce. And some people went for entertainment purposes.

The trip to Wagon Mound took a day to get there and another day to get back so these trips were taken not very often. They would camp in town and there they would bake their own beans in a camp fire. By morning, the beans would be ready. This bean baking was probably the beginning of the Bean Day which started around 1913.

Usually, the Dad and the older siblings went into the village. In Zack's case, he was the oldest son but still too young to undertake such long trips and besides, he had to take care of business at the ranch so his Dad would go by himself. During the course of the year, he would go get the necessities and buy them on credit since money was scarce. The debt would be paid when harvest time came around. Bartering was the common way to go.

The only mode of transportation was on foot, horseback or the horse drawn wagon. In most cases it would be a one horse drawn buggy. Horseback was the most usual type of mobility but very few were the goods that could be carried.

Life in the ranch was easy going and happy were the days spent there even if they had to work hard. Each one had chores to do. There weren't many obstacles or temptations to lure one into trouble.

About the only entertainment they had was to go pray with the penitents at the local morada. There was no church so no priests were available. He doesn't remember ever attending a wedding in this ranch.

Maybe a pass time would be a better description than entertainment. Entertainment has more of a connotation for fun. Praying and specially when kneeling down for long periods of time was any thing but fun. They invented ways to entertain themselves with games which included the farm animals, as well as marbles and base ball.

Zack remembers when he had to carry water from a spring. They had to walk a mile to get the water and woe be the day they had to get bathed. It meant more trips to the spring. Their arms and legs got tired carrying the buckets of water in such a long stretch.

The houses had flat, dirt roofs so when it rained there was no run off to catch the rain. They had to depend on Providence to water their crops and it rarely failed them.

They learned to count by counting their animals and yes, the eggs from the hen house.

At the ripe age of eight or nine years of age, Zack's family had to leave the farm because crops failed and his parents decided to go search for a better life. They moved to Wagon Mound. His father moved the family to a ranch West of Wagon Mound where he raised crops and cows "al partido" with owner, John Paltinghe. "Al partido" means that he shared calves and cows with the owner for his labor, which included taking care of the ranch. The children's horizons expanded and experiences multiplied. A new world had opened for them.

There were four bars, a restaurant, a drug store, some grocery stores, and other buildings such as an opera building. Life became easier to live. There were Anglos and Hispanics living in town. After the ranchers started moving to town, many Anglos bought their land and they moved out to run the ranches.

Zack saw the Yellow Way Buses which, besides the train, was a newer method of traveling. The Yellow Way was the bus which later became the Greyhound Bus. At that time the Yellow Way was a yellow bus hence the name. Later, the Greyhound was gray in color. He was amazed to see so many people from far away places crowed in one vehicle. The bus would stop at Wagon Mound to refuel or so that the passengers would stretch. The train also stopped at Wagon Mound. The train would blow its whistle sometimes at night when everything was quiet and it would wake them up.

In town, they visited the General Stores where everything conceivable at that time, could be found. In these stores, one could buy nails, food, clothing, shoes, coffins and much more. The two General Stores were the Vorenberg and the Macarthur General Mercantile Stores.

The need to learn the value of money became a necessity since candy was available but without money, candy was out of reach unless the parents bought or barter them.

The General Stores dealt with the farmers and ranchers so they all had good trade. Honesty was evident by the handshake and ones word (no written contracts were necessary). People were naive in this time and age. This was the way people were since the times had not advanced to the present form of screwing your neighbor before he screws you. Thank God for the moral values installed in the people's minds. They had no need to lock their doors and be on the look out for robbers. Every one worked for his needs.

Cheaters and crooks were few and far between. If they were caught, they paid dearly so they were very careful not to be caught. When the farmers came to pay their debts, some had more than what they owed and so they splurged or paid in advance. Their faith in being alive the following year was beyond understanding. Some of them splurged on bootleg whiskey.

At school, Zack was surprised to see each grade had a separate room and one teacher to the room. There was a principal as well. Zack had read in English and so he knew his letters and words, however, he did not understand what he was reading.

The school building was a two story building situated in the same grounds where the present school now stands. It housed all grades in the one building. Mrs. Wallenhurst, Mr. Abeyta and a Mrs. Trujillo were the teachers he remembers. Mr. Abeyta was a good math teacher who had an impact on Zack. Aside of having a good math teacher, Zack had a talent so the two facts made him sharp on this subject.

At the Paltinghe ranch, Zack had his chores cut out for him. He sold milk for ten cents a quart which he delivered in a one horse buggy.

His father paid hired hands so that his children could attend school.

When Fort Union was remodeling, they were tearing down old buildings and his dad and Zack brought lumber to build an old outhouse. His father told him that at night he heard the noise as distinct as if it was happening at the time they were tearing the old buildings. They believed that the spirit of the old soldiers came to haunt them.

Zack appreciated and was glad they were poor because that taught him to economize. His father taught him many things that he needed to learn to survive. His father's father died when he was very young and he had to mature fast. He took over as the head of the family.

The teachers, Zack remembers are Mrs. Maude Wallenhurst, Viola Mares and Santiago Abeyta. His high school teachers were Mr. Perry Knight, math and manual training, Mrs. Trujillo was his Spanish Teacher and Mrs. Keys taught other subjects.

One of the high lights Zack remembers in his life was when he had a Mr. Spencer as a teacher. Mr. Spencer had a heck of a time pronouncing his name, Zacarias, and for his benefit he shortened it to Zack. From then on, Zacarias became known as Zack. That is to school personnel because his family kept on calling him Zacarias. To Zack, it was a blessing because his name became shorter and easier to pronounce as well as to write it down.

All through his school career was full of adventures he thought were insignificant. He took Manual Training and other subjects which added to his flexibility. He fooled around with radios, auto mechanics, and many other trades. He did much wood work. He was very creative and there was no end of the many things he could do. He still has furniture he made in his manual training classes. He didn't have time to get bored.

While in high school, he met a beautiful girl who stole his heart the moment he set his eyes on her. She came to school on a bus which brought children from Nolan, a town North of Wagon Mound. As old lady fate would have it, she made her acquaintance with Zack. She was a sophomore and the year was 1932.

Zack, having been struck by cupid's arrow would do anything to be near the object of his affections and so he offered to help her if she ever needed help. Zack was a whiz in math as well as in other subjects. His math knowledge contributed in making him needed. Eloisa Martinez, the object of his distractions, was not too sharp in math or if she was, she led Zack into making her work easier in this subject.

Between them, we find a couple who are humorous and likeable. They can take a joke and can dish it out as well. (This couple was born for each other. Author's words.) Eloisa told this author that she didn't specially care for him but she needed help in math and on other subjects so she humored the lovesick Zack. The matter of truth is that she was as much in love with Zack as he was with her.

Eloisa attended school in Springer which was closer to her home. This move made it harder for Zack but that didn't keep him from traveling the 14 miles to see her at Nolan. She graduated from the Springer High School in 1934 when he was teaching at Mogotes. By now Zack had a 1925 Model T. Later on he bought himself a 1927 Chevrolet.

An incident that happened to Zack when he was still in high school and needs to be presented in this writings is when he was working in a filling station. He had an uncle who cussed like a sailor. He had a Model A car and he constantly chewed tobacco. He would have his window down so as to spit it out. One can imagine how the outside of his car looked. He saw it one day and decided that he needed to have it washed. He took it to the station where Zack worked.

Zack, wanting to impress his uncle did the best job he knew how and when he finished, he raised the window. The car was immaculate clean. Both parties were very proud and happy that the car looked like new. The proud uncle was so grateful that he even tipped Zack and praised him to high heaven and drove off.

Not long after his uncle had taken leave, Zack saw a dust cloud drifting towards him and he wondered what caused the cloud since there was no wind blowing. He didn't have to wait long when he saw his uncle in his Model A and he was a different person that had been there a few minutes before. Zack, smiling and jingling his tip in his pocket, met his uncle and asked him how he could help him. His uncle asked him why in the hell he had closed his #@% window in the driver's side knowing fully well that that window was supposed to be opened all the time. What happened is that uncle had always chewed tobacco and was so accustomed to spitting out that the spit landed in his face. Zack noted his uncle's face kind of brown and so figured why his uncle was angry. His uncle left in a hurry mumbling and Zack was grateful he didn't have to relinquish the tip.

In 1933, Zack graduated from "Wagon Mound High School. He went into teaching the first year at the age of nineteen years of age and nine quarter hours of college to his credit. He taught at Mogotes, a settlement a few miles from Wagon Mound. He started with 25 and up to 30 students. He enjoyed teaching so he decided this would be his vocation.

His father and his mother were firm believers in education so they were ready to help him out if he would keep up his education. He decided that he would attend the Normal University at Las Vegas (now New Mexico Highlands University).

He went back to teaching. He taught at Mogotes for two years then for one year at El Canon de los Manuels near Ocate. After that he was transferred to Watrous.

After his first year of teaching, he bought himself his first car, a Model T. The years passed but his affection for his beloved girlfriend didn't. The trips to Springer were getting to be a drag so he realized he needed a companion.

In 1938, after many trips to Nolan, and putting his pride and bashfulness in his back pocket, he got the nerve to propose to Eloisa. Her mother and the rest of her family loved Zack and they all put in a good word for him so Eloisa playing hard to get finally accepted the proposal of marriage. She told me that at that time she had accepted the proposal to get her revenge. Some time before the proposal, Zack had gone to her house while she wasn't home and her brother had given Zack two of her pet lambs. She was furious but never asked him to return them and exchange them for two of the ugliest ones.

That is what Eloisa told me but that the truth was that she wanted with all her heart to marry him and wondered what took him so long.

The date for their wedding was set and so they went to talk with the priest. On December 25th Christmas day they got married at 1 o'clock. They had a big meal and after the meal they went home. There was no dance and no celebration. Zack's weakness was that he couldn't dance and then he wasn't interested in learning that art. This talent he did not have must be the only talent he doesn't posses.

They went to Denver on their honeymoon. As I was told, when they were close to Pueblo, Zack asked her if they should sleep there or keep on going to Denver. Eloisa answered "You know we are married and we can go all the way". The meaning to that statement was ambiguous and, modest and bashful as he was drove on to Denver.

This beautiful union was blessed with three daughters and a son, namely, Clara, Mary Ellen, Nora and Charles. All of whom went to college and got their degrees. Mary Ellen spent much of her time in Washington D.C. Clara and Nora became teachers who followed their parent's footsteps and Charlie got his degree in Electrical Engineering.

As stated before, Zack taught for the Mora County Schools at Los Manueles, Mojotes, Optimo and other places, until 1937 when the politicians wanted a contribution for their political activities and Zack was in no mood to pay for his teaching privileges and so told them what they could do with their job. That ended the time he worked for the Mora County School System for the time being.

He returned to Wagon Mound somewhat disappointed but his luck changed. He met Mr. Wood who was the Superintendent of the Wagon Mound Municipal School and was searching for a teacher. He didn't have to ask Zack twice if he would like a job teaching at his school. One of his teachers had gotten into trouble and was not hired. Mora County Schools had lost one of the best teachers in their system. Wagon Mound had gained a good math, history, Spanish and social studies teacher. His assignment was the fifth grade.

The United States entered the Second World War when the Japanese bombed Pearl Harbor on December 7, 1941.

In 1942, Zack being of draft age was greeted by President Franklin Delano Roosevelt and cordially invited him to join the armed service. He was a bit reluctant in joining the war. He hated to leave his wife and his profession but he loved his country and when duty calls, Zack is always ready. He joined the U.S. Army in August of that year. His training was a big plus. He had taken Radio school at the New Mexico Highlands University.

He was assigned to Miami Beach, Florida at Camp Murphy close to West Palm Beach. Later he was sent to Macon, Georgia, where he was assigned to teach a contingency of Chinese students. How he managed is his secret since he knew no Chinese and all his students didn't know English.

His next assignment was at Ft. Monmouth, New Jersey where he taught radar. Later he was transferred to Ontario, Canada to study British Air Born Radar. Later on he was sent to Camp Pine Dale, California to await overseas duty. This was in 1944. As old lady fate would have it, he was there in 1945 when the atomic bomb was dropped in two different cities in Japan. The first one did not make the Japanese snap but the second one did and so the war ended.

In January 1946, Zack was sent to Roswell then to Denver where he was Honorably Discharged. And so he came home where his family was, anxiously, awaiting him.

When he returned from serving his country, he reentered New Mexico Highlands University where he used his G.I. Bill of Rights to finish his college degrees.

In 1947, he earned his B.A. degree. By now he was better off in life and he bought a house in Las Vegas.

About this time this author was starting out, recently married and attending college under the G.I. Bill of Rights. Zack had bought his house 3 years before and it was vacant.   He would not rent his house but he loaned it to this author. He would accept no rent so the author felt he had to reciprocate and asked him how he could help him. Zack had a Mercury automobile and it needed brake shoes so he told the author about his troubles with it.   The author had had many previous experiences in doing such work. Both characters went to the part store to buy brake fluid after the shoes had been installed. The brake fluid came in different containers. Some cans were small and some larger that is some were a pint and others a quart. The little cans were in one shelf and the larger ones were in another shelf. The little can would not be enough and the author wanting to expedite grabbed a quart can next to the small cans and took off without noticing what he had picked since the cans looked alike. After the job was finished it was discovered that the big can of fluid contain fire extinguisher fluid it was too late because the fluid was in the system. It was more expense for Zack but he took into account the condition of the author and forgot to mention what had happened until much later.

While going to college, Zack found time to do some radio announcing in the only radio station KFUN, in town. He announced the Spanish Program for some time. This author and one of his friends, naïve as they were, thought that Zack did not have enough people dedicating songs in his program so as to keep him busy, these two would dedicate songs every day. He was patient enough to do them the favor.

Later he returned to teaching as Principal at the Ocate Consolidated School. This was with the Mora County Schools. A different Board of Education had taken place and Zack had better relations with it. He taught there for two years.

He returned to Wagon Mound Schools, where they needed a math, history, and Spanish teacher. Zack fit this slot perfectly.

In 1952 He earned his M.A. degree and kept on teaching at Wagon Mound Schools.

In 1954 he was elevated to the position of Principal and he held that position until 1965 when the previous superintendent, Pete Santistevan, resigned. Zack was offered that position. Zack would never refuse when it came to helping his community and so, graciously, accepted the position. He served in this position until he retired in 1972.

He remembers many of his students who later gave him thanks for teaching them what knowledge they had acquired especially in math.

He had many experiences in dealing with human nature. He recalls when four girls got into a fight. Since he rarely spanked students, he gave them a choice. They could go home and bring their parents or they could tell him what the problem was and then shake hands and everything would be forgotten. He knew that the parents would not give them a choice and at that time parents believed in strict discipline. They made the wise decision to shake hands and be friends.

He has enjoyed his retirement ever since. He and his wife have done extensive traveling. When their son-in-law got in to the exchange of teachers, he went to England with him.

Both, he and Eloisa have traveled to Rome, Washington D.C. Belgrade and many of the states in the U.S.A.

When their son was working as an electrical engineer in California, they made many frequent visits to be with him.

Zack and his wife became much more involved with the Catholic Church and in 2001; they were honored for 20 years of commitment to an area marriage enrichment program. They were presented with a Nambe Sweetheart Bowl to honor them. Father Bennett J. Voorhies and a team presented this award at the St. Anthony's Parish in Pecos.

Among other honors, Zack has received is the Education's Hall of Fame which was presented to him on April 13, 1973.

Later on, I will include copies of the letters of many people who recommended him to the Hall of Fame Committee. Mostly because I believe they do a better job of describing Zack than I could ever. I agree wholeheartedly that all of them knew him better as and unbiased group.

Zack gave me highlights of his life after retiring from school work. To be more precise, I will quote him:

HIGH LIGHTS OF MY LIFE AFTER RETIRING FROM SCHOOL TEACHING

I was very much into the Churches Cursillo Movement, a ministry that was very strong for several years. It started in Spain and came to the U.S. about the middle 1950's. I lived my first Cursillo weekend in 1961. It was the third Cursillo that took place in this area.

A Cursillo is a concentrated religious course that lasts three days. This weekend was held at the remaining army barrack at Camp Luna. The team was made up of Spanish speaking men from San Antonio Texas so it was all in Spanish.

After that I continued participating as a team member and gave several talks called "Rollos" on various topics on evangelization.

On February 1981, I got a call from Albert and Josephine Garcia from Immaculate Conception in Las Vegas to tell me about a marriage enrichment program. It is also a ministry where couples make up the weekend team and gave talks on various topics on marriage, dealing mainly with their own experience as a married couple. Eloisa and I lived our first marriage enrichment weekend on February 11-13-, 1981 in Las Vegas. We were then invited to give a talk at our Lady of Guadalupe in Peralta, New Mexico. This, our very first talk was on the topic of "Marriage, a Sacrament".

On that same year in November, we were asked to help at I.C. in Las Vegas where we gave the talk on "Joys of Marriage".

After working a few more weekends on Marriage Enrichment, we found that our efforts were most rewarding. Not only did it re-enforce our own marriage, but the most fulfilling result was the influence that we had on numerous other couples, where in some cases, we feel that we saved their marriage. Many couples had so much faith in our marital example that wanted to know our secret for such a good marriage example. This is evident by the great number of cards and letters we have received from couples that feel grateful for the way we touched their lives.

Several couples who were asked to give a weekend talk wanted our opinion to give a final O.K. on their talk to see if it was the way it was supposed to be. One particular couple, Manuel and Rachel Garcia, from Risen Savior Parish in Albuquerque called and read us long distance from Albuquerque to Wagon Mound to ask us to hear their talk so that we could criticize it. It made us most happy to be asked for such confidential favor.

In the process of working so many weekends, 103 in all, through April 2002, we have become very close to hundreds of couples, not only as friends but in many cases, like family. We, affectionately, refer to all Marriage Enrichment weekenders as our Marriage Enrichment family.

We add a lot of humor to our talks and with the humor try to put across a point. An example I like to use is when trying to emphasize the importance of the Catholic Marriage. Once you are married by the Catholic Church you can never legally separate. The story goes about a couple that mutually agreed to separate and went to see a priest. They asked, "Father would it be possible for us to separate? We both agreed that we do not love each other any more". Father answered, "Yes, I think we can arrange it, please follow me". They followed the priest to a side room with very dim lights and he told the couple to kneel down. Father grabbed a small vessel with holy water and picked up a heavy stick and dipped it in the holy water and hit the man on the head with it. He did the same with the lady. This went on a few times, dipping the stick in holy water and hitting each one in turn. After a while their heads were aching pretty much so they asked the priest, "How long is this going to go on?" and the priest answered, " Until one of you dies!". So marriage is until God do us part."

I wish it were possible to remember all the good people we meet in Marriage Enrichment Weekends. It's so embarrassing when we meet someone at the store or anywhere and they say, "Howdy Mr. and Mrs. Montoya," and neither of us recognizes them. They remember us but we don't recall them. I like to blame it on my age, and that way I get away with it. It is a fact that when you get to be fifty years of age, you forget names: when you get to 60 you forget faces: when you get to 70 you forget to put up your zipper: and when you get to 80, you forget to put your zipper down.

Sometimes to put emphasis on friendship that is built during weekends, I like to tease Paul Maes, a friend I met on the very first weekend we worked at Peralta, New Mexico, Our lady of Guadalupe Parish, I say that Paul has become such a good friend of mine that there is nothing he wouldn't do for me, and there is nothing, but nothing I wouldn't do for him so it happens that we spend a lot of time doing nothing for each other. We always find it tactful to, when giving a talk it helps to get the full attention of all present at the very start. My popular one has been that I get very nervous in front of an audience and it reminds me of my first date: "I didn't know where to put my hands!" Eloisa always breaks in with:" It didn't take him long to know where to put them!"

When we celebrated our 60th wedding anniversary, a lot of people had many nice complements about us. At one point, Eloisa turned to me and said, "I am proud of you". Being so hard of hearing, I asked her, "What?" Then she repeated a little louder: "I'm proud of you!" Then I said, "Oh, I'm tired of you too!"

I asked Zack that if he had his life to go back, what changes he would make. His answer was that he would not make any changes. If he had to go back and serve Uncle Sam, he would do it again willingly. He says that he has no regrets in life, and knowing him, he means it. That's Zack.

I will continue Zack's story by including the statements of different people while recommending him for the Education Hall of fame.

".. *Along the Santa Fe Trail* .."

Springer Municipal Schools

FRED J. POMPEO, SUPERINTENDENT

P. O. BOX 308   PH. 483-2662

Springer, New Mexico 87747

January 30, 1973

Mrs. Marjorie N. Monette
Chairwoman, Hall of Fame
Wagon Mound Public Schools
Wagon Mound, New Mexico 87752

Dear Mrs. Monette:

I am pleased to recommend Mr. Zack Montoya as a candidate to the Hall
of Fame.

Zack's contributions to his school, to his community, and to education
have been outstanding during the some thirty years he has been
associated with the Wagon Mound Schools.

Mr. Montoya has been and continues to be one of my friends. He is one
with whom others willingly associate. I recommend him, without
reservation, for this well-deserved honor.

Sincerely,

Fred J. Pompeo

Fred J. Pompeo

January 31, 1973
Mora, New Mexico

Mrs. Marjorie N. Monette,
Chairman, Hall of Fame
Wagon Mound Education Association
Wagon Mound, New Mexico 87752

Dear Mrs. Monette:

It is indeed a great honor and a privilege to recommend
Mr. Zack Montoya's candidacy to the Hall of Fame.

Many times I had wished I could work in the same system
with Mr. Montoya. The opportunity presented itself in the
1970-71 school term. Mr. Montoya approached me and offered
me the principalship of the Wagon Mound School system and
although, I had my position in the Mora Independent School
system, I accepted.

For two years, I worked side by side with Mr. Montoya. I
came to know Mr. Montoya as a patient, unbiased, just,
conscientious, and hard working man.

I know he was envolved, as he still is, in all community
activities that take place in that town.

If I have seen Mr. Montoya angry, I have not been able to
detect him. He keeps his composure and controls his tongue
well.

I know that if anyone needs help and he is able to help, he
will go out of his way to help friends and strangers alike.

The decisions I have seen him make(many of which were very
hard and some I did not agree with at the time) have proved
to be right.

When he had to let some teachers go, he was as diplomatic as
could be. There were no hard feelings.

How much Mr. Montoya has contributed to the education of all
our youngsters cannot be measured but I am sure that history
will reveal his worth in time.

All of Mr. Montoya's former students and people I have met
praise him highly.

I have met many fine educators who deserve to be in the Hall
of Fame. Of all of these fine people, I do not know who is
more deserving of this honor than Mr. Montoya. I am positive
that all who have really known Mr. Montoya will agree with me
wholeheartedly.

Without reservations, I recommend Mr. Montoya as a candidate
to the Hall of Fame not only of the Northern District but the
State and Nation.

Sincerely yours,
Manuel B. Alcon

14

BERNALILLO PUBLIC SCHOOLS

P.O. Box640 · Bernalillo, New Mexico 87004 · 505 867-2317

January 31, 1973

Mrs. Marjorie N. Monette
Chairman, Hall of Fame
Wagon Mound Education Assoc.
Wagon Mound, New Mexico 87752

Dear Mrs. Monette:

I appreciate your recent letter informing me that the Wagon Mound
Education Association plans to nominate Mr. Zack Montoya as a
candidate to be placed in the Hall of Fame in the Northern District.

The membership of the WMEA is to be complimented for their efforts
in nominating Mr. Montoya to the Hall of Fame. I believe that Mr.
Montoya's service to the Wagon Mound Public School and to our state
is unparalleled. Very few educators have the commitment to education
and the children displayed by him over the thirty years he served in
the profession.

Mr. Montoya's leadership in education will be missed as well as his
leadership in the community of Wagon Mound.

I strongly endorse the action of the WMEA in nominating Mr. Zack
Montoya to the Hall of Fame. I certainly recommend him for this
great honor.

Respectfully yours,

Pete Santistevan
Superintendent

PS:sp

15

February 1, 1973

To Whom It May Concern:

It is a distinct pleasure to recommend Mr. Zack Montoya for candidacy to the teachers' Hall of Fame.

He has served School District #12 in varied capacities, executing the duties of each office to the utmost of his ability.

His record regarding community affairs is one of action and concern. He has always been deeply involved in civic matters.

Perhaps Mr. Montoya can best be characterized by saying that he incorporates, among other traits, a friendly manner and a true sense of Christian decency toward his fellow men.

I am confident that all the people of the area unite with me in endorsing this man without reservation.

Respectfully,

C. R. Monette

C. R. Monette
Box 7
Wagon Mound, New Mexico

February 1, 1973

To whom it may concern:

I am very pleased to hear that Mr. Zack Montoya has been nominated as a candidate for the N. M. E. A. Hall of Fame. In all sincerity I don't know of a person more deserving of that honor, and greater honors. As long as I have known Mr. Montoya, his concern for the youth in the small communities in New Mexico was to be admired. He was never satisfied that they should have an education, but the best education possible. I have the greatest respect for Mr. Montoya as an educator and school administrator.

Mr. Montoya's talents are without number. He was, and, I'm sure that he still is, ready to help anyone in need. I find Mr. Montoya to be an outstanding Christian. I'm sure that his "charity in action" has been a tremendous influence on his students as well as others who came in contact with him. Mr. Montoya's ability to do many things well was a tremendous help to me when I was pastor of Santa Clara Parish in Wagon Mound.

I feel that it is an honor for me to have known and have worked with Mr. Montoya, in Parochial affairs, and that he considers me to be a close friend. In a way its a shame that Mr. Montoya has ended his teaching career instead of just beginning it. I pray that God will bless us with more concerned and dedicated educators like him.

Yours sincerely,

Rev. Anthony P. Bolman
Pastor of St. Rose of Lima Parish
Santa Rosa, New Mexico

STATE OF NEW MEXICO

DEPARTMENT OF EDUCATION ⸺ EDUCATION BUILDING

SANTA FE — 87501

LEONARD J. DE LAYO
SUPERINTENDENT OF PUBLIC INSTRUCTION

February 2, 1973

TO WHOM IT MAY CONCERN:

I heartily endorse the nomination of Mr. Zack Montoya to the Hall of Fame.

I have known Mr. Montoya for many years and have worked with him in my capacity as Director of School Transportation since 1966. It has been my observation that he has provided dedicated leadership in the community which he served for many years and has constantly strived to improve opportunities for the children of Wagon Mound.

In an area of declining pupil enrollment, he, as Superintendent, has faced many difficulties and, in my opinion, made his decisions on a factual, professional basis.

Public education in New Mexico is indebted to Mr. Zack Montoya for his long, dedicated service in the Wagon Mound Schools.

Sincerely,

C. B. Lemon, Director
SCHOOL TRANSPORTATION DIVISION

CBL:bjb

417 Mora Ave.
Raton, New Mexico
February 2, 1973

Mrs. Marjorie Monette, Chm.
Hall of Fame Committee
Wagon Mound, New Mexico

Dear Mrs. Monette:

It is indeed a pleasure to write a letter recommending
Mr. Zack Montoya as a candidate for membership in the Northern
District, NEA-New Mexico Hall of Fame.

My knowledge of and professional work with Mr. Montoya
extends over a period of approximately twenty-five years.
In that time Mr. Montoya has repeatedly aided the teaching
profession, and extended leadership to it, by serving as an
officer oraas a member of numerous statewide or district
committees. Always his work with such groups has been that of
a responsible and interested citizen.

While he was superintendent Mr. Montoya repeatedly demon-
strated interest in and concern for the quality of the instructional program of the Wagon Mound Public Schools. During a period
of change in content of the elementary school mathematics program,
Mr. Montoya contrived time to attend each of the workshop sessions
held for the assistance of elementary teachers.

My support of the nomination of Mr. Montoya for Hall of Fame
membership rests on his fine-type professionalism and on his
dedication to a high-quality instructional program for pupils.

Sincerely yours,

Lura Bennett
Lura Bennett

19

February 6, 1973

Mrs. Marjorie N. Monette
Chairman, Hall of Fame
Wagon Mound, New Mexico

Dear Mrs. Monette:

It is a great pleasure and a personal source of pride
to be able to count Mr. Zack Montoya as one of my friends.
Not only has our friendship contributed to many enjoyable
associations, but I have felt strength and inspiration
in our professional association. Zack Montoya is one of
those admirably concerned individuals whose dedication to
education has dignified it above the daily pursuits. He
has made contributions not only by what he has done but also,
and most importantly, by what he has been.

Yes! I am greatly gratified in being able to add one more
recommendation to Zack's inclusion in the Hall of Fame.
Individuals of his stature are few and far between.

Respectfully submitted,

Dr. Willie Sanchez
Assistant to the President
for External Affairs

WS/am

11623 Lexington N. E.

Albuquerque, N. M. 87112

February 6, 1973

Mrs. Marjorie Monette

Wagon Mound Schools

Wagon Mound, New Mexico 87752

Dear Mrs. Monette:

We had the pleasure of working with Mr. Zack Montoya
for nearly twenty-five years, first as co-workers then with
him as our Superintendent of Schools. He is a man of high
principles, concern for others, and deeply religious. He
was never to busy to take part in activities that promoted
the welfare of the students, the teachers, and the parents.

Mr. Montoya was dedicated to the Betterment of Education
and took every opportunity to serve on committees, in programs,
in multi-state groups, and with the North Central Association
to secure that improvement.

He gave freely of his time and outstanding ability to the
community; working many hours over that called for in the
line of duty.

We are proud to recommend Mr. Zack Montoya as a Candidate
to the Hall of Fame.

Sincerely,

Francis Hooven

Mr. & Mrs. Francis Hooven

P·O·BOX 729 · SANTA FE · NEW MEXICO · 87501
TELEPHONE 505·982·1916

February 6, 1973

Ms. Marjorie N. Monette
Chairman, Hall of Fame
Wagon Mound, New Mexico 87752

Dear Ms. Monette:

It is with pride and confidence that I recommend Mr. Zack Montoya
as a candidate to be placed in the Hall of Fame in the Northern District.

I have known Mr. Montoya for a good many years and have worked
closely with him while I was in Raton Schools and with the State Department of Education.

Mr. Montoya is intelligent, energetic and a dedicated Educator. He
is ethical and extremely capable individual who has served the community
of Wagon Mound for over thirty years.

Mr. Montoya is known and respected both locally and state-wide. I
am sure the Educators of the Northern District couldn't make a better
choice.

Sincerely,

Charles B. Sweeney,
Business Manager

CBS:ab

717 Sperry Drive
Las Vegas, New Mexico 87701
February 6, 1973

Mrs. Marjorie N. Monette
Chairman, Hall of Fame Committee
Wagon Mound Education Association
Wagon Mound, New Mexico 87752

Dear Marjorie:

Zack Montoya was born and raised in Wagon Mound and was educated in the Wagon Mound Public Schools. With the exception of his first years of teaching, all his years in public school service were given to the Wagon Mound Schools.

He has served the school in all capacities from a class room teacher to the Superintendent. Each change he made in the school was a step up the ladder in school responsibility and obligations. This is indicative of his ability and devotedness to his profession as well as the confidence the Board of Education had in Mr. Montoya and his ability.

Mr. Montoya gave to the best of his abilities in all school work and projects. He also was associated with many Community projects. He is a member of the Santa Clara Catholic Church and an ardent worker in all phases of church work. He was Chairman of the American Red Cross in Mora County for many years. For this he gave of his time and efforts without any fanfare and little if any recognition. Here we see a man interested in helping mankind through a worthwhile organization. Mr. Montoya was involved in the Bean Day Association projects as well as many other Community things

Mr. Montoya is a man of high moral character and is well liked and respected in the school and the community.

Sincerely

Bertha P. Dettmann
Mrs. Arthur V. Dettmann

January 8, 1973

Zack Montoya
Wagon Mound, New Mexico 87752

Dear Zack:

Enclosed you will find copies of the certificates which you designed for us as they look after we have completed the printing. I thought you would be interested in seeing them.

We certainly appreciate your help in putting these certificates together. Sincere thanks.

Sincerely,

Edmund A. Gaussoin
Executive Secretary

EAG:as

National Education Association of New Mexico

This Certifies That

_____

Has been elected to serve on the commission for term which

begins _____ and ends _____

Dated at Santa Fe, New Mexico _____ 19___

_____
President - NEA - New Mexico

_____
Executive Secretary

Education's

HALL OF FAME

Northern District

New Mexico Education Association

presented to:

Zach Montoya

This certificate is presented in appreciation and recognition of long and faithful service to the teaching profession.

Presented this _13th_ day of _April_, _1973_

CHAIRMAN HALL OF FAME COMMITTEE

PRESIDENT NORTHERN DISTRICT

THE UNIVERSITY OF NEW MEXICO | ALBUQUERQUE, NEW MEXICO 87106

DEPARTMENT OF MODERN AND CLASSICAL LANGUAGES
TELEPHONE 505: 277-5907

February 10, 1973

Mrs. Marjorie N. Monette
Chairman Hall of Fame
Wagon Mound, New Mexico, 87752

Dear Mrs. Monette:

I am indeed very happy to be able to recommend Mr.
Zack Montoya as a candidate whose name is to be placed in
the Hall of Fame of your district.

I have known Mr. Montoya for the past thirty years
or so and have always known him to be a quiet, hard-work-
ing individual.

Mr. Montoya's integrity and leadership in his community are of the highest. His service in the field of education has made him widely known and admired by everyone
he comes into contact with.

It is with a great deal of pleasure then that I add
my recommendation to the many others that this young man
is getting in his favor for the Hall of Fame.

Very sincerely yours,

Rubén Cobos
Associate Professor of Spanish
Dept. Of Modern and Classical Langs.

February 10, 1973

To Whom It May Concern:

I have known Mr. Zack Montoya for a lifetime and have found him to be one of the community's most outstanding citizens.

He willingly extended a helping hand in whatever way he could and was especially kind and understanding to children.

I feel certain that all who know him well join with me in supporting him for the New Mexico Education Association's Hall of Fame.

Yours truly,

Chas G. Nelson

Charles G. Nelson

Charles G. Nelson
P. O. Box 248
Wagon Mound, New Mexico

Wagon Mound High School
Wagon Mound, New Mexico 87752
February 13, 1973

To whom it may concern:

Concern is a simple word used everyday by most everyone. As
common as this word is, though, few include it as part of their
philosophy.

One person who has made it a part of his philosophy is
Mr. Zack Montoya. Concern is a force that has played an
important role in his life. Because of his concern for
humanity, he has had a fulfilling career. The concern he
expresses for his family has resulted in his having a hard
working family also dedicated to education. His friends can
also be attributed to his concern.

Fortunately, I was able to share one year of his career with
him. This was his last year; it was my first. Because of his
background, his knowledge, and his experience, I was able to
learn many things from him from ordering books to developing film.
His positive attitudes were communicable. His patience and
understanding were encouragement. His willingness to assist in
solving problems was relieving.

Unfortunately, this lasted for one year. He is greatly missed
as superintendent of Wagon Mound High School. A visit with him
on occasion finds him working on a project, remodeling his house,
or planning a trip.

Although his role has changed, he is still the same inspiring
man. During his farewell speech at graduation last May he said
to the students, "You are all my children. If there is anything I can do to help, never hesitate to contact me. . ." It
is obvious that this force, concern, will be with him forever.

Although I have known him for such a short time in comparison to
others, I find this man to have many traits that are fast becoming
extinct in our society. A man such as this who has dedicated his
life to education deserves to be honored and recognized.

Yours truly,

Miss Geraldine Lujan
Business Teacher

February 14, 1973

TO WHOM IT MAY CONCERN:

I have known Mr. Zack Montoya for the last thirty years.
I knew him as a teacher, principal, and school superintendent.

As a teacher, he was greatly admired by his students. He
treated them kindly and did his utmost to guide and prepare them
for a successful life.

As principal and school superintendent, he respected the
dignity of each and every individual. He was very considerate
of his co-workers, administrators and students.

He is a highly moral person, and a good christian. He
has been very active in social and church affairs. He served
in the church council for many years, and has contributed his
help in numerous church activities as well as many community
activities.

I with the rest of my fellow teachers, appeal for your
support of our candidate, Mr. Zack Montoya, to the Hall of
Fame.

Sincerely,

Audilia DeTevis

Mrs. Audilia DeTevis
Second Grade Teacher

February 14, 1973

Having worked with Mr. Montoya for 25 years I feel he
has the qualities that make him worthy of having his name
placed in the Hall of Fame.

We who have worked in a like capacity can appreciate
Mr. Montoya's patience, courage, amiable disposition, ability
to get along with people, and his integrity.

Viola C. Isbell

Viola Isbell

February 16, 1973

Mrs. Marjorie N. Monette
Wagon Mound Public Schools
Wagon Mound, New Mexico

Dear Mrs. Monette,

I have known Mr. Zack Montoya during most of my school years. He is very respectful and cooperative. He is always willing to help you in everything.

Mr. Montoya is a great man to imitate he always has a kind word for everyone. I admire him very much.

I recommend him to the Hall of Fame.

Yours truly
Benito Mondragon Jr.

February 16, 1973

Mrs. Marjorie N. Monette
Wagon Mound Public Schools
Wagon Mound, New Mexico

Dear Mrs. Monette,

One of the good things in my life is
having known Mr. Zack Montoya. Mr. Montoya is
a very respectful, kind, generous and understanding person. He has a great and wonderful
family whom I know are very proud of him.

My first contacts which brought me to
knowing Mr. Zack Montoya were during my High
School years. He was my Spanish and History teacher.
He was really as great a teacher as they come
and somehow he was always so kind and cheerful.
If for some reason you were feeling low, you'd
walk into his classroom he'd greet you with
a cheerful smile and a little joke and that
would really brighten your day. Somehow that
great spirit of his would get into all of us.
I'm sure he doesn't know how many times he
turned my bad days to good days just by
being himself.

In recent years I've again had the big

opportunity to converse with Mr. Zack Montoya during one of our religious activities and I find he's still the same great Mr. Montoya; in spite of his tasks in life which I'm sure he has had; he is still the kind of person that makes you want to be like him. He's so willing to give and give and be of help to everyone. Everyone in our family respects, admires and thinks the world of Mr. Zack Montoya for he is not only a good person, a great teacher but also a good Christian.

Therefore, I would like to recommend Mr. Zack Montoya to the Hall of Fame.

Yours truly,
Celina Mondragón

February 16, 1973

Marjorie N. Monette
Hall of Fame Chairman
Wagon Mound, N.M. 87752

Dear Hall of Fame Committee:

As one of the many young people from Wagon Mound who attended its public schools and are presently enjoying some success in life, I would like to attribute my success to people like Zack Montoya. He dedicated his life's work to guiding and encouraging students to better themselves.

My initial contact with Zack was when he taught World History. While he conducted his class with a firm hand, he indeed put across his material to the class, at least he did to me.

Later, Zack became principal of the high school. During his tenure, he became involved in numerous co-curricular activities, like the Camera Club where he taught his students to develop film. He was even our bus driver for our senior trip to Juarez. I can remember nothing but pleasant events about his leadership while I was in high school. I didn't appreciate things be did for us then until I became an educator and realized how time consuming these activities were.

Recently, my professional contact with the Wagon Mound Public Schools has been in actively recruiting students to the University of New Mexico. During these trips I've talked and gotten to know Zack more professionally the last two years of his superintendency than ever before. I've realized that his leadership has kept the school in good standing, as far as the State of New Mexico and North Central Association are concerned. On the other hand, I've overheard or being told by people who have visited the school that they were impressed with the well-kept facilities and the healthy learning environment in the classrooms.

I haven't lived in Wagon Mound since 1955 when I graduated from high school, therefore, I don't know about Zack's involvement in community services. But, comparatively speaking, if his educational endeavors are anything like his community service, there is no doubt in my mind that he had and is still having a positive impact on the community.

It is with great pride and honor that I recommend to you Mr. Zack Montoya who has given his most productive years to the community of Wagon Mound in all facets of life.

Sincerely yours,

Gilbert G. Montoya
Gilbert G. Montoya

February 16, 1973

Mrs. Marjorie N. Monette
Wagon Mound Public Schools
Wagon Mound, New Mexico

Dear Mrs. Monette,

I have known Mr. Zack Montoya
during most of my school years. He
is very respectful and cooperative.
He is always willing to help you
in everything.

Mr. Montoya is a great man to
imitate he always has a kind word for
everyone. I admire him very much.

I recommend him to the Hall
of Fame.

Yours truly,
Benito Mondragon Jr.

36

February 17, 1973

Mrs. Marjorie N. Monette
Wagon Mound Public Schools
Wagon Mound, New Mexico

Dear Mrs. Monette,

     I have known Mr. Zack Montoya all my life. Mr. Montoya has always been a respectful citizen and he is always willing to help each and everyone; whether your need be of school, community, or religious origin. He is never too busy to listen to and understand the problems of others. Mr. Montoya is a close friend of mine as well as my Godfather. He is a very reliable person and I respect and admire him very highly.

     I would like to recommend Mr. Zack Montoya to the Hall of Fame.

Sincerely,
Robert Mondragón

March 22, 1973

To Whom It May Concern:

This is a most difficult task. It is very hard to express our feelings about daddy because words are just not adequate. To be a poet or songwriter maybe would help and yet, I wonder. To communicate such deep devotion is very hard. I know that when I'm finished with this letter it will not even begin to cover everything that we feel about him. Nobody can understand unless they have known him as a father or husband. Those who have worked with him possibly could begin to understand the kind of person he is. I shall just do the best I can.

He is unlike any other man. He is the perfect husband and father. Any flaws in his character have never been evident to us. He is unselfish and a man of great faith. Everything that we have ever accomplished in our lives has been with this foremost thought in mind: to please daddy. He has never let us feel as though we were being judged. He has never pushed us, only inspired through example. He is always there when we need him. He is a model that I hope my children will emulate. He is objective, openminded and yet the most loving person I know. I think that we must be the luckiest family in the world to have such a wonderful father.

Sincerely,

Nora Montoya Juarros

CITIZENS STATE BANK OF SPRINGER

WAGON MOUND, NEW MEXICO

February 23rd, 1973

To Whom it may concern:

I have known Mr. Zack Montoya for many years
He has always taken an active part in all civic work,
Church work and his outstanding work in our Public
School certainly merit great consideration in the
Hall of Fame.

Sincerely

Beulah Farquer
Assistant Vice President & Manager

March 26, 1973

To whom it may concern:

There are no words that I could possibly say that would
begin to express my sincere feelings for or about this
man. What can be said about a person who has lived and
dedicated his work toward making a better future for his
family, associates, and friends? A person such as this
can be better described by his own deeds.

Mr. Zack Montoya is a very special person. He not only
is involved in one area of interest, but in several projects in the community and state. If anybody at any time
needs something, from an electrician, to a photographer;
or, just plain advise from a friend, Mr. Montoya is always willing to lend a helping hand. Many people, who
have been in contact with him, will attest to the fact
that Mr. Montoya has a certain way with people and a
heart big enough for anybody in need. One only has to
see how people respect this man to realize what kind of
person he is. He has always set an example of what one
must do in this life to achieve success and happiness.
All that one must do is reflect upon what Mr. Montoya
has accomplished and how he has gone about it, and follow it as a guideline. If anybody accomplishes half as
much as Mr. Montoya has, he will truly be a success.

Personally, I know that I will never be able to accomplish
as much as this man, or have a personality such as his;
nevertheless, I will always strive to be like him. The
most important thing to me, above all that can be said
or has been said, is that he is my dad and I love him
very much.

Respectfully submitted,

Carlos R. Montoya
Carlos Romulo Montoya

March 5, 1973

TO WHOM IT MAY CONCERN:

I worked under Mr. Zack Montoya from September 1970 through May 1972 for the Wagon Mound Public Schools. During this time I was responsible for setting up a four area pre-vocational education program which included drafting, wood-work, metalwork and electricity.

Mr. Montoya provided the administrative support needed to implement this program. I believe his concern for the students' needs in the vocational education area will have a great impact in their future.

Sincerely yours,

Meliton Maestas, Teacher
Pre-Vocational Education

March 1, 1973

TO WHOM IT MAY CONCERN:

I have known Mr. Zack Montoya since I was a child.
As far back as I can remember, he was always involved with
the school, church, and community.

During my high school years at Wagon Mound School, Mr.
Montoya was my math teacher and principle. It was to my
advantage that Mr. Montoya was such an excellent teacher
for he prepared me for future math classes.

Later, I came back to the Wagon Mound School to teach
and had the pleasure of working under his guidance. Mr.
Montoya always had a kind word of encouragement. He was
always willing to help me professionally or personally.

I sincerely believe that a man of such high regards
for education and people in general should definitely be
nominated to the Hall of Fame.

Sincerely yours,

Susan S. Medina

Susan S. Medina
Third Grade Teacher

March 4, 1973

TO WHOM IT MAY CONCERN

It has been my good fortune to have served for a number of years as a teacher under Mr. Zack Montoya when he was superintendent of the Wagon Mound Schools. I won't say how many years, as I wouldn't care to stir up any undue speculation as regards my age; however, I wish to assure you that the period of time was more than ample to become well acquainted with Mr. Montoya's capabilities as an administrator and with his worth as a responsible member of the community.

Mr. Montoya was worked unceasingly to raise the standards of our school both in academic achievement and in classroom behavior. In regard to discipline he was always fair but firm, meting out just and impartial punishment for undesirable conduct. He was a friend to the students as well, and all felt the stabilizing effect of his guidance at some time or other throughout their school careers.

Mr. Montoya is a man of quiet strength and true greatness whose character is unimpeachable. I strongly urge that he be placed in the Hall of Fame.

Respectfully yours,

Marjorie Monette

(Mrs.) Marjorie Monette

March 5, 1973

TO WHOM IT MAY CONCERN:

I have known Mr. Zack Montoya in many capacaties - teacher principal - and superintendent. I am pleased to recommend him as a candidate to the Hall of Fame.

This man possesses many qualities which would appear necessary for this type of honor - leadership·integrity - honesty - loyalty - patience and humbleness. He is a very religious man and an outstanding christian.

Mr. Montoya has always given unstintingly of his time and talent to further any worthy educational cause, and has cheerfully and willingly worked without thanks or compensation on numerous church and civic projects.

Although he is now retired his "pride and joy" is still the Wagon Mound School. The employees and students of the·Wagon Mound School will always be sure of his help and advise on whatever they might·need.

Sincerely,

Angie Sandoval

Angie Sandoval
School Secretary

April 4, 1973

To Whom It May Concern:

   Knowing a person who is patient, understanding beyond the
highest expectations and always available for sincere advice
is extremely fortunate. Mr. Zack Montoya is such a person and
has been so to many people. The greatest blessing of all is to
have this wonderful person as my father. It is difficult to
put into words the many things my father has done for me but
I am very greatful. With the deepest love and admiration, I
can truly say I am my father's daughter.

                              (Mrs.) Clara Garcia

Whom It May Concern:

ne, a dear, momentous aspect of life, has a way of passin g
'ore we realize it has. Time brings with it various associa-
ns, memories and personalities, among other things. One
'son I recall in association with the word <u>time</u> is Mr. Zack
itoya.

Montoya has always had the time for people, no matter what
: need. As I search my memory, I recall many a time when I
ild turn to no one else, personally or professionally, but
. Montoya -- and he always had the time to listen, consider,
:n console, if that were called for. Yet, I was only one
'son, and there were more, many more who sought his time. He
iays gave it, gladly, graciously, courteously, sincerely.

Montoya's time was and is still given in such manner -- to
: family, his church, his friends, his community, his fellow
i, in general.

I had to think back on my life and choose a list of persons
), I feel, have influenced positively my professional as well
my personal ethics, Mr. Zack Montoya's name would be very
;h on that list.

is my honest and sincere opinion that Mr. Zack Montoya is
rery sincere and conscientious man and that he is worthy of
:ry and any consideration for this honor.

(Mrs.) J. L. Gonzales

To the Wagon Mound School Faculty (Present & Past)

Last Friday, May 22, our daughter received her High School Diploma at the
Graduation exercises. She is the last of our five children to graduate
from Wagon Mound High School. We estimate (roughly) that you have offered
them 63,000 hours of your time and knowledge. I (the mother) have been
around school for many years and we know for fact that they've caused you
many headaches - our apologies for that. We know for a fact that some of
you have given them some sore bottoms - our thanks to you for that. As
parents we have probably given some of you a hard time by sticking up for
our little stinkers, not realizing we have become immune to their smell -
our apologies for that, also. What you have taught them we will list as
intangible for not even they will ever fully realize how much you have done
for them in that respect. What we do know is that their accomplishments are
to be credited to you.

We gave (loaned, is a better word) you five children to help us raise and to
educate (from their Headstart or Primary years through their senior years) and
we are very satisfied with what you did with them and to them. We will not
venture to state or even guess which teacher did the most for each child because we know that each one of you had a hand in educating and the molding of
their characters. Our sincere thanks to everyone of you.

Sincerely yours,

Paul & Olivia Herrera

Paul and Olivia Herrera
(one set of satisfied parents)

*This letter
is a good example of
how some parents feel about
school. I had many such teaching
experiences in my school days.
Zack*

National Education Association of New Mexico

P•O•BOX 729 • SANTA FE • NEW MEXICO • 87501
TELEPHONE 505•982•1916

November 21, 1973

Mr. Zack Montoya
P. O. Box 67
Wagon Mound, New Mexico 87752

Dear Zack:

You will recall that I discussed with you the designing of a series of certificates for NEA-New Mexico. You indicated that you would be happy to do so if I would indicate what wording I felt was appropriate. I am enclosing the wording for two certificates.

Please use your own good judgement in the design. If you could possibly design a nice border for the certificate, it would be helpful. This should be done so the certificate is on 8 1/2 x 11 paper with black ink.

I hope you are enjoying your retirement. We know you are missed by the Wagon Mound schools and by the profession in New Mexico.

Sincerely,

Edmund A. Gaussoin
Executive Secretary

EAG:as

I thought

you'd like to h

the clipping.....

Dear Zack —

I might be a late — but then it's never too late to let friends know that we are happy for them.

Gordon Lopez was here the other day, & we were both saying how this honor was well deserved.

Regards to the family, & kindest wishes.

Sincerely,

~ Leach

Zack Montoya

Scholarship In Honor Of Zack Montoya

Journal Special

WAGON MOUND — A new scholarship presented to Robert Mondragon at the Wagon Mound High School commencement exercises was in honor of Zack Montoya, retired superintendent with more than 35 years of school service.

The scholarship was presented to young Mondragon by Donald Elmore and Lew Zale, owners of the Diamond Z Ranch. The award will be given yearly to some deserving senior at Wagon Mound.

The scholarship was awarded in honor of Montoya for his long service and dedication to the Wagon Mound school district.

A COLLECTION OF ABSENCES ACTUALLY RECEIVED

1. Dear School: Please excuse John from being absent on January 28, 29, 30, and also 32, and 33

2. please excuse Diane from being absent yesterday. She was in bed with gramps.

3. I had to keep Billie home because she ad to go shopping because I didn't know what size she ware.

4. Please execute Johnny for being. It was his fathers fault.

5. Mary could not come to school because she was bothered by very close veins.

6. Chris will not be in school because he has a acre in his side.

7. John had been absent because he had tow teeth taken off his face.

8. Please excuse Gloria. She has been under the doctor.

9. Lillie was absent from school yesterday because she had a going over.

10. My son is under the doctors care and should not take fiscal ed. Please execute him.

11. Carl was absent yesterday because he was playing football. He was hurt in the growing part.

12. My daughter was absent yesterday because she was tired from spending the weekend with the marines.

13. Please excuse Ray Friday from school. He has very lose vowels.

14. Mary Ann was absent Dec. 11-15 because she had a fever, sore throat, headache, and upset stomack. Her sister was also sick, fever and sore throat, her brother had a low grade fever and ached all over. I was not the best either, sore throat and fever. There must have been the flu going around. Her father even got hot last night.

15. Please excuse Blanche from jim today. She is admnistrating.

16. George was absent yesterday because he had a stomack.

17. Ralph was absent yesterday because of a sore trout.

18. Please excuse Wayne for being out yesterday because she had the fuel.

19. Please excuse Sarah for being absent. She was sick and I had her shot.

Wagon Mound, New Mexico

Zack

Montoya

MARRIAGE ENRICHMENT WEEKENDS

by

Zack and Eloisa Montoya

1	Las Vegas, (IC)	Feb 11-13, 1981	Candidates
2	Peralta, (OLOG)	Apr 24-26, 1981	Marriage a Sacrament
3	Las Vegas, (IC)	Nov 6-8, 1981	Joys
4	San Juan Pueblo,	Feb 12-14, 1982	Joys
5	Las Vegas, (IC)	Mar 26-28, 1982	Co-Leaders (MWG)
6	Las Vegas, (IC)	Oct 1-3, 1982	Leaders (GWG)
7	Wagon Mound, (SC)	Nov 5-7, 1982	Leaders (GWG)
8	Las Vegas, (IC)	Feb 25-27, 1983	Marriage a Sacrament
9	Mora, (St Gertrude)	Sep 23-25, 1983	Joys
10	Las Vegas, (IC)	Nov 6-8, 1983	Man/Woman/God
11	Santa Rosa, (SR Lima)	Nov 18-20, 1983	Joys
12	Portales, (St Helen)	Feb 10-12, 1984	Joys
13	Springer, (St Joseph)	Mar 23-25, 1984	Leaders (GWG)
14	Questa,	Sep 21-23, 1984	Joys
15	Tucumcari, (St Anne)	Feb 15-17, 1985	Joys
16	Ribera, (San Miguel)	Apr 19-21, 1985	Leaders (GWG)
17	Peralta, (OLOG)	Feb 14-16, 1986	Joys
18	Las Vegas, (IC)	May 16-18, 1986	Marriage in Community
19	Wagon Mound, (SC)	Nov 21-23, 1986	Leaders (GWG)
20	Raton, (SP-SJ)	May 1-3, 1987	Leaders (GWG)
21	Tucumcari, (St Anne)	Nov 21-23, 1987	Love & Sex
22	Peralta, (OLOG)	Mar 18-20, 1988	Joys
23	Portales, (St Helen)	May 13-15, 1988	Marriage in Community
24	Albuq., (St Edwin)	Jun 3-5, 1988	Joys (Spanish)
25	Las Vegas, (IC)	Nov 11-13, 1988	Leaders (GWG)
26	Tucumcari, (St Anne)	Nov 17-19, 1988	Marriage a Sacrament
27	Clayton, (St Francis)	Apr 14-16, 1989	Joys
28	Albuq., (Risen Savior)	Nov 3-5, 1989	Marriage a Sacrament
29	Tucumcari, (St Anne)	Mar 23-25, 1990	Love & Sex
30	Las Vegas, (IC)	May 18-20, 1990	Marriage a Sacrament
31	Moriarty, (St Carmel)	Oct 26-28, 1990	Marriage a Sacrament
32	Las Vegas, (IC)	Nov 30-2, 1990	Marriage a Sacrament
33	Albuq., (St Edwin's)	Feb 8-10, 1991	Joys
34	Albuq., (Risen Savior)	Mar 1-3, 1991	Man/Woman/God
35	Las Vegas, (IC)	Sep 28-30, 1991	Children/Fam/Relatives
36	Albuq., (Risen Savior)	Mar 6-8, 1992	Man/Woman/God
37	Las Vegas, (IC)	Apr 3-5, 1992	Marriage a Sacrament
38	Raton, (SP-SJ)	Jun 19-21, 1992	Leaders (GWG)
39	Clovis, (OLOG)	Nov 13-15, 1992	Marriage a Sacrament
40	Las Vegas, (IC)	Nov 20-22, 1992	Marriage a Sacrament

41	Edgewood,	Apr 23-25, 1993	Marriage a Sacrament
42	Albuq., (Risen Savior)	Jul 23-25, 1993	Joys
43	Albuq., (San Martin)	Oct 1-3, 1993	Man/Woman/God
44	Isleta (St Augustine)	Oct 22-24, 1993	Love & Sex
45	Las Vegas, (IC)	Nov 5-7, 1993	Joys
46	Carlsbad, (St Joseph)	Feb 25-27, 1994	Marriage a Sacrament
47	Estancia,	Mar 11-13, 1994	Marriage a Sacrament
48	Las Vegas, (IC)	Apr 8-10, 1994	Christian Marriage
49	Ribera, (San Miguel)	May 13-15, 1994	Marriage a Sacrament
50	Raton, (SP-SJ)	Jun 17-19, 1994	Joys
51	Albuq., (Risen Savior)	Jul 22-24, 1994	Marriage a Sacrament
52	Las Vegas, (IC)	Sep 23-25, 1994	Children/Fam/Relatives
53	Isleta, (St Augustine)	Oct 21-23, 1994	Communication
54	Albuq., (San Jose)	Feb 10-12, 1995	Joys (Spanish)
55	Albuq., (Risen Savior)	Mar 3-5, 1995	Man/Woman/God
56	Las Vegas, (IC)	Mar 24-26, 1995	Communication
57	Moriarty, (St Carmel)	Mar 31-2, 1995	Communication
58	Ribera, (San Miguel)	Apr 21-23, 1995	Joys
59	Albuq., (Risen Savior)	Jul 21-23, 1995	Joys
60	Albuq., (San Jose)	Sep 8-10, 1995	Joys (Spanish)
61	Isleta, (St Augustine)	Oct 20-22, 1995	Joys
62	Albuq., (St Edwin's)	Oct 27-29, 1995	Joys
63	Carlsbad, (St Joseph)	Nov 10-12, 1995	Marriage a Sacrament
64	Grants, (St Teresa)	Feb 2-4, 1996	Communication
65	Peralta, (OLOG)	Feb 9-11, 1996	Love & Sex
66	Ribera, (San Miguel)	Mar 15-17, 1996	Children/Fam/Relatives
67	Las Vegas, (IC)	Mar 22-24, 1996	Communication
68	Albuq., (Risen Savior)	Mar 29-31, 1996	Man/Woman/God
69	Rio Rancho, (T. Aquinas)	Jul 19-21, 1996	Joys
70	Albuq., (Risen Savior)	Jul 26-28, 1996	Marriage a Sacrament
71	Albuq., (Holy Rosary)	Nov 22-24, 1996	Man/Woman/God
72	Carlsbad, (St Joseph)	Feb 14-16, 1997	Children/Fam/Relatives
73	Los Lunas, (San Clemente)	Mar 7-9, 1997	Joys
74	Ribera, (San Miguel)	Mar 14-16, 1997	Marriage in Community
75	Las Vegas, (IC)	Apr 4-6, 1997	Joys
76	Rio Rancho, (T. Aquinas)	Apr 25-27, 1997	Joys
77	Albuq., (Risen Savior)	Jul 25-27, 1997	Children/Fam/Relatives
78	Albuq., (St Anne's)	Sep 19-21, 1997	Marriage a Sacrament
79	Las Vegas, (IC)	Oct 17-19, 1997	Marriage a Sacrament
80	Albuq., (Risen Savior)	Nov 7-9, 1997	Joys
81	Peralta, (OLOG/St Clem.)	Mar 6-8, 1998	Children/Fam/Relatives
82	Albuq., (Holy Rosary)	Mar 20-22, 1998	Joys
83	Albuq., (San Martin)	Apr 24-26, 1998	Understanding of Self
84	Albuq., (Holy Family)	May 15-17, 1998	Joys
85	Albuq., (Risen Savior)	Jul 24-26, 1998	Man/Woman/God
86	Ribera, (San Miguel)	Sep 18-20, 1998	Marriage in Community

87	Moriarty, (St Carmel)	Oct 16-18, 1998	Understanding of Self
88	Rio Rancho, (T. Aquinas)	Oct 23-25, 1998	Children/Fam/Relatives
89	Carlsbad, (St Joseph)	Feb 12-14, 1999	Love & Sex
90	Los Lunas, (San Clemente)	Mar 5-7, 1999	Joys
91	Pecos, (St Anthony)	Mar 19-21, 1999	Children/Fam/Relatives
92	Clovis, (OLOG)	Mar 26-28, 1999	Love & Sex
93	Albuq., (St Edwin's)	Apr 16-18, 1999	Communication
94	Fountain, CO(St Joseph)	Aug 6-8, 1999	Joys
95	Ribera, (San Miguel)	Sep 10-12, 1999	Understanding of Self
96	Rio Rancho, (T. Aquinas)	Sep 17-19, 1999	Love and Sex
97	Albuq., (St Edwin's)	Oct 8-10, 1999	Joys
98	Peralta, (OLOG/St Clem.)	Mar 3-5, 2000	Love and Sex
99	Pecos, (St Anthony)	Apr 7-8, 2000	Communication
100	Los Lunas, (San Clem.)	Mar 2-4, 2001	Communication
101	Pecos, (St Anthony)	Mar 30-31, 2001	Joys
102	Albuq., (Holy Rosary)	Nov 2-4, 2001	Joys
103	Los Lunas, (San Clemente)	Apr 12-14, 2002	Joys
104	Clovis, (OLOG)	Apr 19-21, 2002	Love & Sex
105	Las Vegas, (IC)	Apr 26-28, 2002	Communication
106	Pecos, (St Anthony)	May 3-6, 2002	Marriage in Community
107	Belen, (OLOB)	Oct 18-20, 2002	Marriage in Community
108	Los Lunas, (San Clemente)	Mar 14-16, 2003	Children/Fam/Relatives
109	Las Vegas, (IC)	Mar 28-30, 2003	Love and Sex
110	Socorro, (San Miguel)	Apr 25-27, 2003	Joys
111	Las Vegas, (IC)	Sep 19-21, 2003	Marriage in Community
112	Belen, (OLOB)	Oct 17-19, 2003	Love & Sex
113	Santa Fe (St Francis)	Nov 14-16, 2003	Love & Sex
114	Socorro, (San Miguel)	Feb 14-16, 2004	Love & Sex
115	Las Vegas, (IC)	Feb 20-22, 2004	Marriage in Community
116	Taos (OLOG)	Apr 23-25, 2004	Joys
117	Las Vegas, (IC)	Sep 17-19, 2004	Marriage in Community
118	Clovis, (OLOG)	Nov 12-14, 2004	Communication
119	Ribera, (San Miguel)	May 13-15, 2005	Marriage in Community
120	Las Vegas, (IC)	Nov 04-06, 2005	Joys
121	Socorro, (San Miguel)	Feb 17-19, 2006	Joys
122	Los Lunas, (San Clemente)	Mar 03-05, 2006	Joys
123	Las Vegas, (IC)	Mar 24-26, 2006	Marriage a Sacrament
124	Belen, (OLOB)	Oct 13-15, 2006	Love & Sex
125	Las Vegas, (IC)	Nov 10-12, 2006	Christian Marriage
126	Taos, (OLOG)	Mar 16-18, 2007	Man/Woman/God
127	Los Lunas, (San Clemente)	Mar 23-25, 2007	Love & Sex
128	Las Vegas, (IC)	Apr 27-29, 2007	Marriage Partner
129	BELEN (OLOB)	OCT 19-21, 2007	LOVE & SEX
130			

WEEKEND BREAKDOWN

Locations/Total		Weekends/Year	Talks/Total	
Las Vegas	29	1981-3	Leaders(GWG)	8
Peralta	6	1982-4	Co-Leaders	1
San Juan	1	1983-4	Man/Woman/God	9
Wagon Mound	2	1984-3	Communication	10
Mora	1	1985-2	Child/Fam/Rel	8
Santa Rosa	1	1986-3	Love & Sex	17
Portales	2	1987-2	Joys	39
Springer	1	1988-5	Christian Mar	2
Questa	1	1989-2	Mar in Community	10
Tucumcari	4	1990-4	Mar a Sacrament	21
Ribera	8	1991-3	Und. of Self	3
Raton	3	1992-5	Mar Partner	1
Albuquerque		1993-5	TOTAL	127
Risen Savior	12	1994-8		
St Edwin's	5	1995-10		
San Martin	2	1996-8		
San Jose	2	1997-9		
Holy Rosary	4	1998-8		
St Anne's	1	1999-9		
Clayton	1	2000-2		
Moriarty	3	2001-3		
Clovis	4	2002-5		
Edgewood	1	2003-6		
Isleta	3	2004-5		
Carlsbad	4	2005-2		
Estancia	1	2006-5		
Grants	1	2007-3		
Rio Rancho	3			
Los Lunas	7			
Pecos	4			
Socorro	3			
Belen	3			
Santa Fe	1			
Taos	2			
Fountain, CO	1			
TOTAL	128			

ZACK AND ELOISA MONTOYA' 60TH WEDDING ANNIVERSARY

NO SMOKING PLEASE

One of my bygone recollections,
As I recall the days of yore,
Is the Little House, behind the house,
With the Crescent over the door

'Twas a place to sit and ponder,
With your head bowed down low;
Knowing that you wouldn't be there,
If you didn't have to go.

Ours was a three holer,
With a size for every one.
You left there felling better,
After you usual job was done.

You had to make these frequent trips
Whether snow, rain, sleet, or fog-
To the Little House where you usually
Found the Sears-Roebuck catalogue.

Oft times in dead o winter,
The seat was covered with snow,
'Twas then with much reluctance,
To the Little House you'd go.

With a swish you'd clear the seat,
Bend low, with dreadful fear,
You'd blink you eyes and grit you teeth,
As you settled on your rear.

I recalled the day my Granddad,
Who stayed with us one summer,
Made a trip to the Shanty,
Which proved to be a "hummer."

'Twas the same day my dad
Finished painting the kitchen green.
He'd just cleaned up the mess he made
with rags and gasoline.

He tossed the rags in the shanty hole,
And went on his usual way,
Not knowing that by doing so
He would eventually rue the day.

Now Granddad had an urgent call,
I never will forget!
This trip he made to the Little House,
Lingers in my memory yet!

He sat down on the Shanty seat,
With both feet on the floor,
Then filled his pipe with tobacco,
And struck a match on the outhouse door.

After the tobacco began to glow,
He slowly raised his rear,
Tossed the flaming match in the
Open hole, with no sign of fear.

The blast that followed, I am sure,
Was heard for miles around;
And there was poor ol' Granddad
Just sitting on the ground.

The smoldering pipe was still in his mouth,
His suspenders he held tight;
The celebrated three-holer
Was blown clear out of sight!

When we asked what happened,
His answer I'll never forget.
He thought it must be something
That he had recently "et!"

Next day we had a new one,
Which my Dad built with ease.
With a sign on the entrance door
Which read: !No Smoking, Please."

Now that's the end of the story,
With memories of long ago,
Of the Little House, behind the house,
Where we went 'cause we had to go!

(Submitted for the humor to those of us
that have taken that long walk)

Before Marriage

After Marriage

Two Temples

A builder builded a temple
    He wrought with care and skill
Pillars and groins and arches
    Were fashioned to meet his will
And men said when they saw its beauty
    "It shall never know decay
Great is thy skill O Builder
    Thy fame shall endure for Aye".

A Teacher builded a temple
    He wrought with skill and care
Forming each pillar with patience
    Laying each stone with prayer
None saw the unceasing effort
    None knew of the marvelous plan
For the temple the teacher builded
    Was unseen by the eyes of man.

Gone is the builders temple
    Crumbled into the dust
Pillars and groins and arches
    Food for consuming rust
But the temple the teacher builded
    Shall endure while the ages roll
For that beautiful unseen temple
    Was a child's immortal soul.

                —Hattie Vose Hall

ABOUT THE AUTHOR

HIGH LIGHTS ON THE LIFE OF MANUEL BENJAMIN ALCON Jr.

Born :September 18, 1926

Parents: Benjamin Alcon De Buck and Rosaura Montoya to a family of six sisters and Manuel..

Birth Place: Ocate, New Mexico

Schools attended: Wagon Mound Public School- Primary grade Wagon Mound, New Mexico
 Mora Elementary. Mora, New Mexico

High school: Mora High School. Mora, New Mexico

   Clayton High School-Freshman year. (Clayton, New Mexico).

Drafted: 1944 United States Navy . Served in the amphibious force aboard the USS LST 54 in the Atlantic Ocean during the Normandy Invasion and was Discharged Honorably 1946.

   Reenlisted Navy Reserve 1947. Discharged Honorably 1954

Colleges: New Mexico Highlands, Las Vegas, New Mexico GED1947, B.A-1955 M.A.1958

   Attended Columbia University 1963 workshop in Administration, New York, NY.

   New Mexico State University workshop in Administration, Las Cruces,N.M.

   Other workshops at University of New Mexico. Albuquerque, N. M.

   Attended workshops at New Mexico University at Las Cruces,

Experience in Education: Teacher: Monte Aplanado- one room school 1952 Mora, County

   Schools. 26 students from kindergarten through eighth grade.
   Holman Consolidated School Holman, N.M.1953-1955 also 1958.

   West Las Vegas Elementary School Las Vegas, NM 1955-1957.

   Elementary Principal at Mora Elementary. 1959-60.

   Elected Mora County Schools Superintendent. 1960

   Appointed Mora Independent School Superintendent 1961-1965.

   Returned to Classroom at Guadalupita 1965-1968.

   Principal at the Mora High School 1968-1971

   Principal at the Wagon Mound Municipal Schools 1971-1973.

   Mora High school History teacher 1973- Principal until Retirement in 1985.

Accomplishments: Last functional Superintendent of the Mora County Public Schools.

   First Functional Superintendent of the Newly formed Mora Independent Schools.

   Appeared in: LEADING MEN IN THE UNITED STATES 1965

   PERSONALITIES OF THE WEST AND Mid West 1968

   MOST ADMIRED MEN &WOMEN OF THE YEAR 1994

Awards: District Teacher of the year 1978

   U.S. Naval Training Center Alumnus 1985.

   Some trophies from different organizations such as the St. Gertrude Credit Union

   Charter member of St. Gertrude Credit Union -Served as treasurer, Supervisory Committee chairman and President .

   Charter member of Post #114 American Legion -served in most positions as also in

District 1as Commander twice and also as Sargeant at arms.

Charter member of VFW Post #1131- served as Commander, quartermaster, adjutant, Judge advocate and in District 5 as Chaplain.

Basketball trophy 1955 and others.

Hobbies: Wood work carving, hiking, reading, writing. Three of my works have been published

Authored a booklet on the life of Levi Madrid - "LEVI MADRID MORA'S PATRIARCH" In 1990

Authored a book on the History of Mora titled "LO De Mora". Published _ 2005.

Published some stories in Las Vegas Daily Optic, Mora Communicator and in books published by other authors.

TODAY

Outside my window, a new day I see
and only I can determine
what kind of day it will be.
It can be busy and fun, laughing and gay
or boring and cold,
unhappy and grey.
My own state of mind is the determining
key, for I am only the person
I let myself be.
I can be thoughtful and do all I can
to help, or be selfish and think
just of my self.
I can enjoy what I do and make it seem
fun, or grip and complain
and make it hard on someone.
I can be patient with those who may
not understand,
or be little and hurt them as much as I can
But I have faith in myself,
and believe what I say,
and I personally intend to make
the best of each day.